Showtunes

ISBN 0-634-06956-X

HAL•LEONARD®
CORPORATION
7777 W. BLUEMOUND RD. P.O. BOX 13819 MILWAUKEE, WI 53213

Visit Hal Leonard Online at
www.halleonard.com

Bali Ha'i

from SOUTH PACIFIC

Electronic Organs
Upper: Flutes (or Tibias) 16', 4'
      String 8'
Lower: Flutes 8', 4'
Pedal: String Bass
Vib./Trem.: On, Fast

Drawbar Organs
Upper: 60 3616 113
Lower: (00) 7634 212
Pedal: String Bass
Vib./Trem.: On, Fast

Lyrics by Oscar Hammerstein II
Music by Richard Rodgers

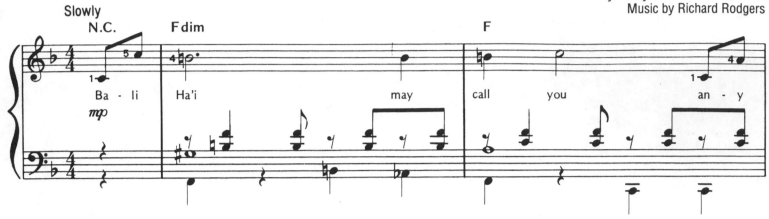

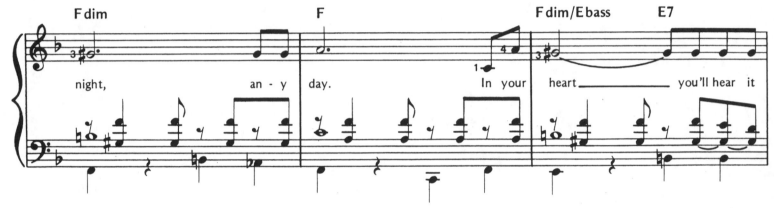

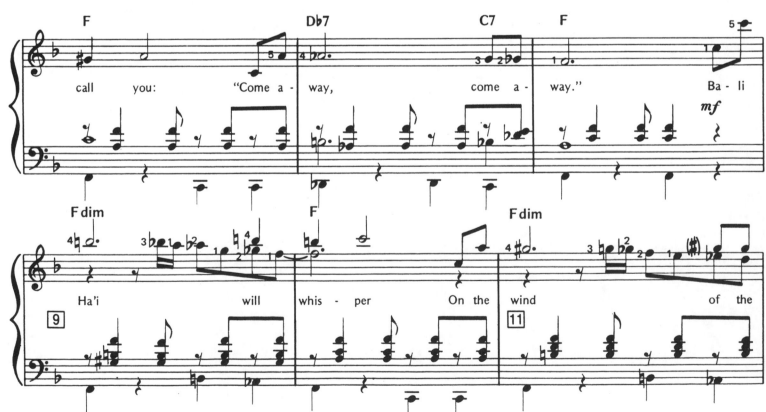

Bewitched

from PAL JOEY

Electronic Organs
Upper: Flutes (or Tibias) 16', 4',
       String 8'
Lower: Flutes 8', 4', Diapason 8'
Pedal: String Bass
Vib./Trem.: On, Fast

Tonebar Organs
Upper: 60 3616 113
Lower: (00) 7634 212
Pedal: 54
Vib./Trem.: On, Fast

Words by Lorenz Hart
Music by Richard Rodgers

Dm7   D♭7   C   E7   F6   Fdim

would-n't sleep   when   love came and   told me I   should-n't sleep,   Be -

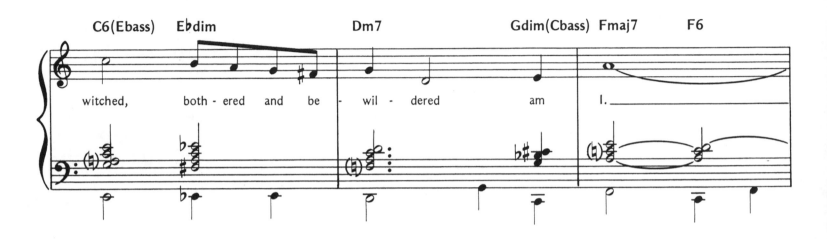

C6(E♭bass)   E♭dim   Dm7   Gdim(Cbass)   Fmaj7   F6

witched,   both - ered and be - wil - dered   am   I. _____

Em7   A7   Dm(Gbass)

Both Hands *8va* -

Lost my heart,   but what   of   it?

Both Hands Upper

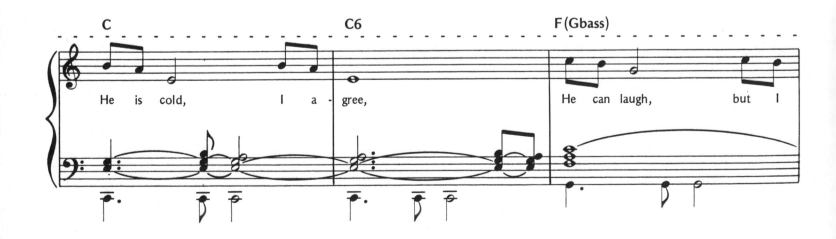

C   C6   F(Gbass)

He is cold,   I a - gree,   He can laugh,   but I

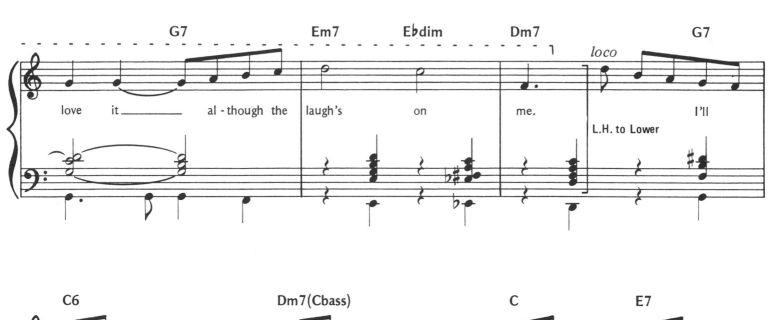

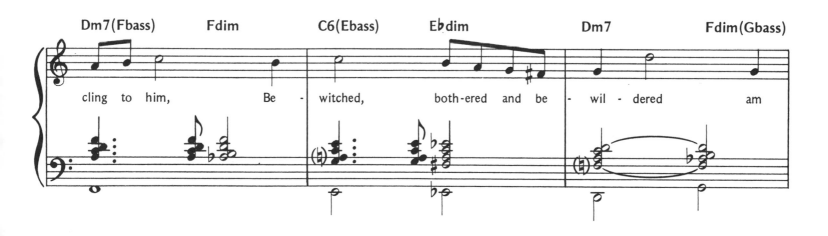

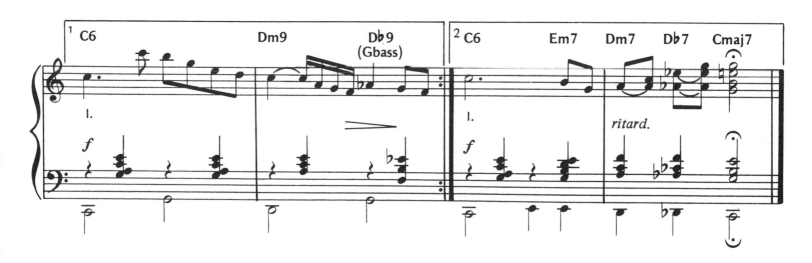

Blue Skies

from BETSY

Electronic Organs

Upper: Flutes (or Tibias) 8', 2', Clarinet
Lower: Flute 4', Diapason 8', String 8'
Pedal: String Bass
Vib./Trem.: On, Fast

Drawbar Organs

Upper: 00 8383 833
Lower: (00) 5555 330
Pedal: String Bass
Vib./Trem.: On, Fast

Words and Music by
Irving Berlin

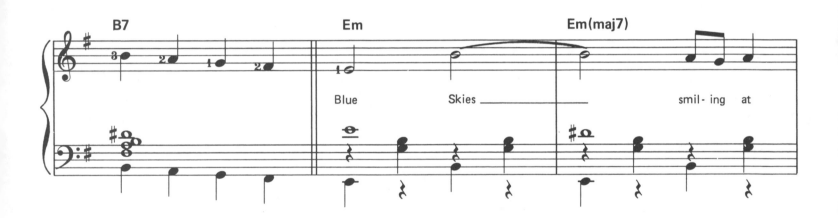

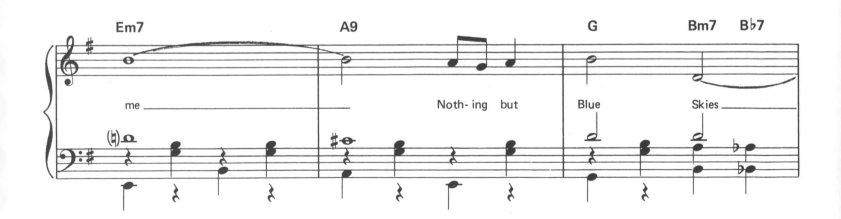

9

Button Up Your Overcoat

from FOLLOW THRU

Electronic Organs
Upper: Flutes (or Tibias) 16′, 8′, 5⅓′, 4′
Lower: Flutes 8′, 4′, Diapason 8′
Pedal: 8′, Sustain
Vib./Trem.: On

Drawbar Organs
Upper: 88 6600 000
Lower: (00) 8760 000
Pedal: 55 String Bass
Vib./Trem.: On

Words and Music by B.G. DeSylva,
Lew Brown and Ray Henderson

Easy swing

Cabaret

from the Musical CABARET

Electronic Organs
Upper: Flutes (or Tibias) 16', 4'
         Trombone, Trumpet
Lower: Flute 8', Diapason 8', Reed 8'
Pedal: String Bass
Vib./Trem.: On, Fast

Drawbar Organs
Upper: 82 5864 200
Lower: (00) 7103 000
Pedal: String Bass
Vib./Trem.: On, Fast

Words by Fred Ebb
Music by John Kander

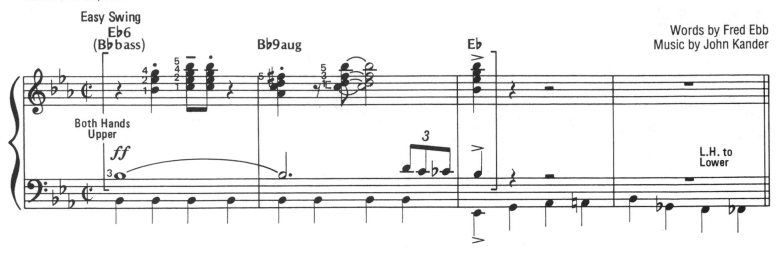

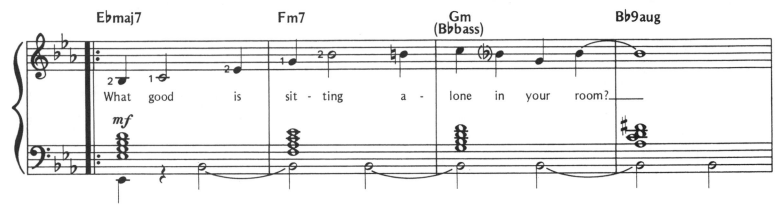

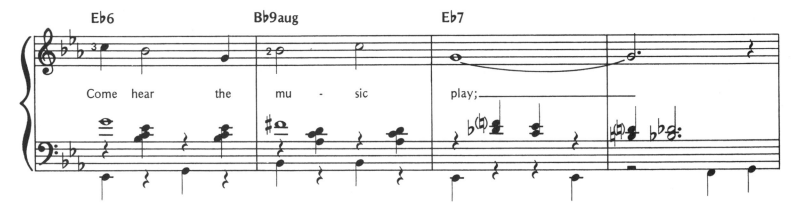

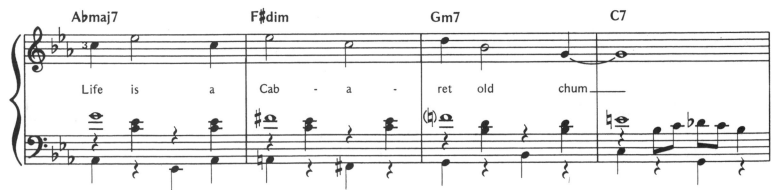

Camelot

from CAMELOT

Electronic Organs

Upper: Flutes (or Tibias) 8', 2'
Lower: Flute 8', String 8'
Pedal: String Bass
Vib./Trem.: On, Fast

Drawbar Organs

Upper: 00 6007 000
Lower: (00) 5004 000
Pedal: 42
Vib./Trem.: On, Fast

Words by Alan Jay Lerner
Music by Frederick Loewe

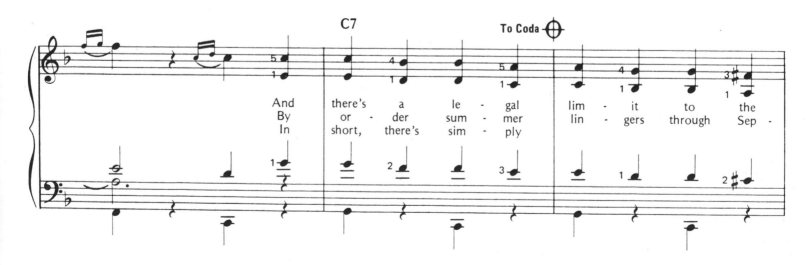

Easter Parade

from AS THOUSANDS CHEER

Electronic Organs
Upper: Flutes (or Tibias) 16', 4'
          String 8', Clarinet
Lower: Flutes 8', 4'
          String 8'
Pedal: 16', 8'
Vib./Trem.: On, Fast

Tonebar Organs
Upper: 80 8104 103
Lower: (00) 6303 004
Pedal: 25
Vib./Trem.: On, Fast

Words and Music by
Irving Berlin

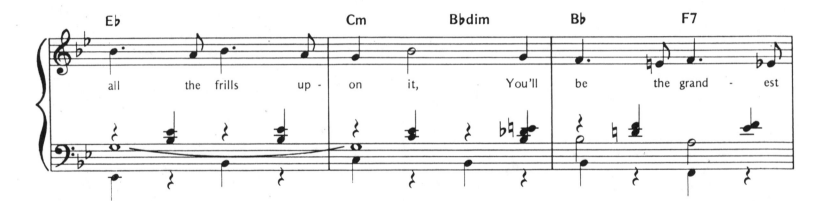

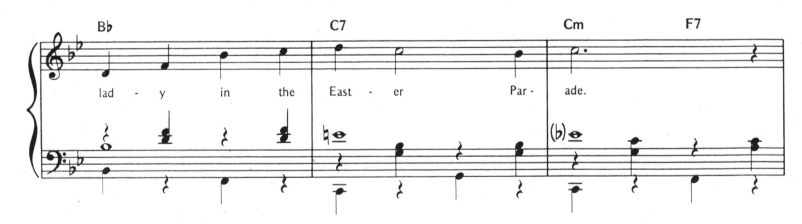

Falling in Love with Love
from THE BOYS FROM SYRACUSE

Electronic Organs

Upper: Flutes (or Tibias) 16', 8'
       String 8'
Lower: Flute 8'
       Diapason 8'
Pedal: 8'
Vib./Trem.: On, Fast

Tonebar Organs

Upper: 60 3616 200
Lower: (00) 7634 212
Pedal: 24
Vib./Trem.: On, Fast

Words by Lorenz Hart
Music by Richard Rodgers

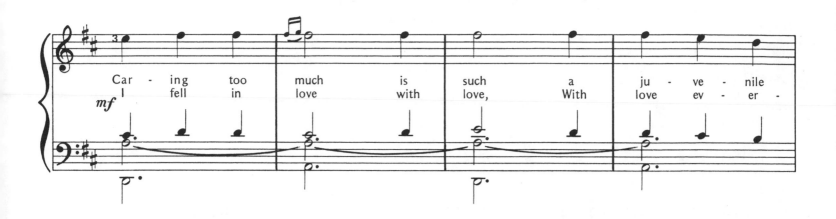

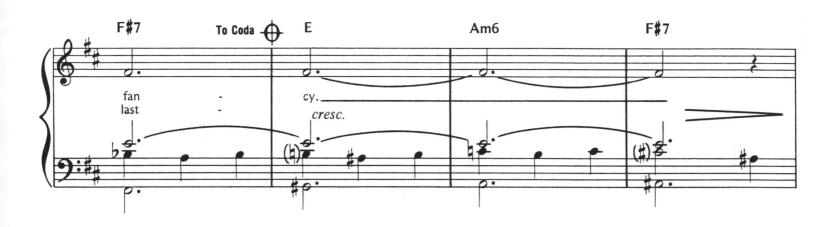

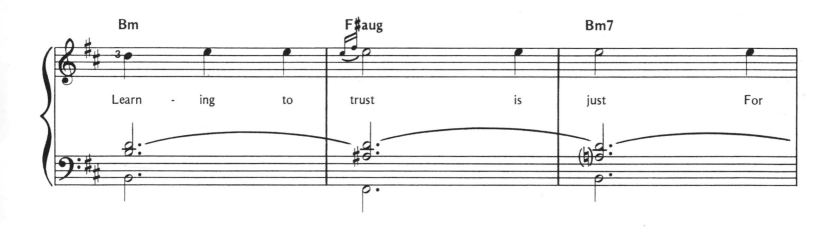

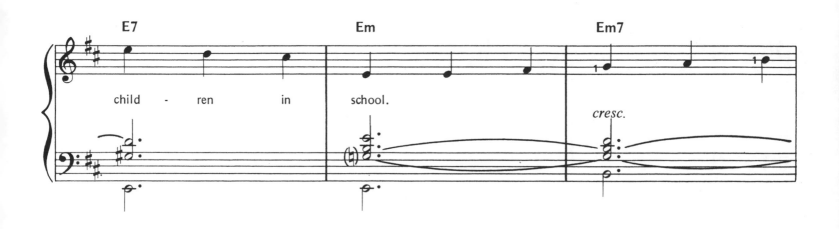

Edelweiss

from THE SOUND OF MUSIC

Electronic Organs

Upper: Flute (or Tibia) 4'
     Sustain
Lower: Flute 8'
Pedal: 8'
Vib./Trem.: On, Fast

Drawbar Organs

Upper: 00 0600 000
Lower: (00) 7000 000
Pedal: 05
Vib./Trem.: On, Fast

Lyrics by Oscar Hammerstein II
Music by Richard Rodgers

Slowly
R.H. 8va to end

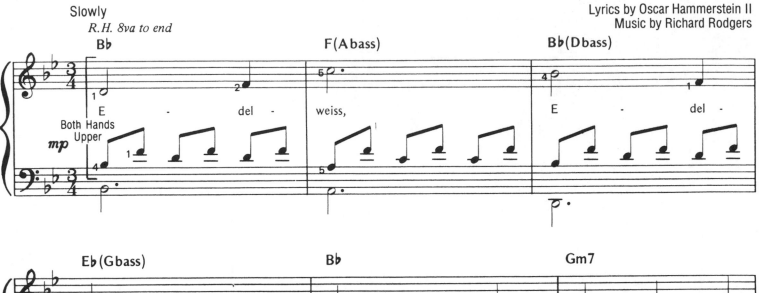

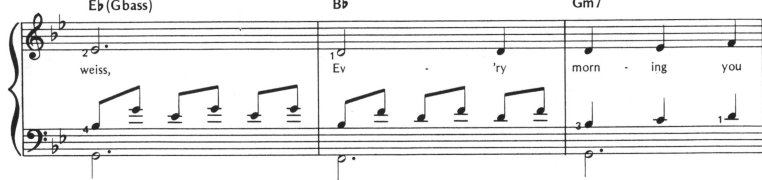

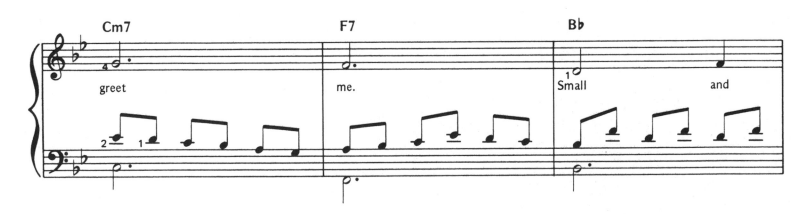

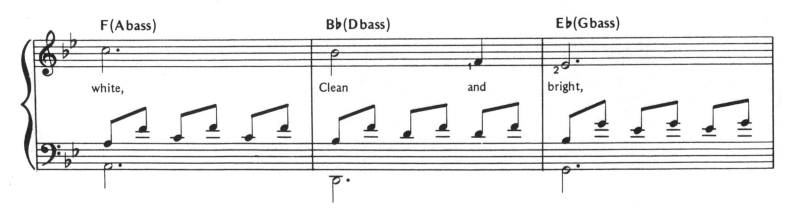

Get Me to the Church on Time

from MY FAIR LADY

Electronic Organs
Upper: Flutes (or Tibias) 16′, 8′, 4′
       Trumpet, Oboe
Lower: Flutes 8′, 4′
       String 8′, Reed 8′
Pedal: 16′, 8′
Vib./Trem.: On, Fast

Tonebar Organs
Upper: 80 7766 008
Lower: (00) 8076 000
Pedal: 37
Vib./Trem.: On, Fast

Words by Alan Jay Lerner
Music by Frederick Loewe

Moderately Fast

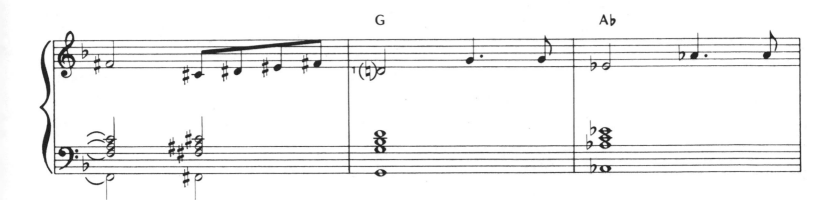

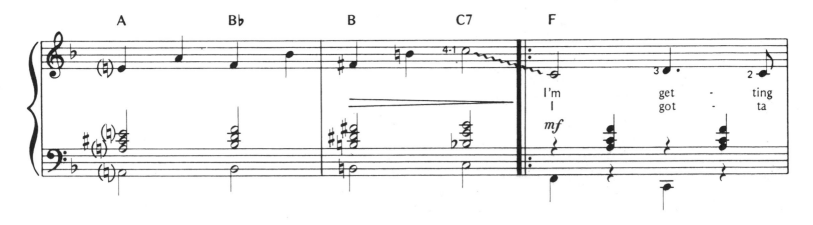

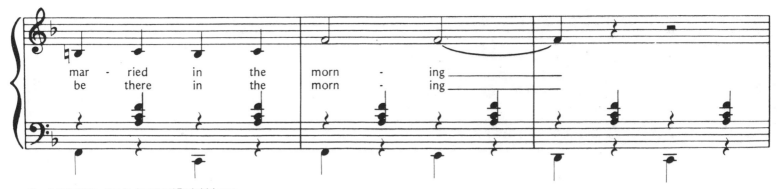

Getting to Know You

from THE KING AND I

Electronic Organs

Upper: Flutes (or Tibias) 16', 8', 5 1/3', 4' or
Trombone
Lower: Flutes 8', 4', String 8'
Pedal: String Bass
Vib./Trem.: On, Fast

Drawbar Organs

Upper: 83 6030 400
Lower: (00) 6402 003
Pedal: String Bass
Vib./Trem.: On, Fast

Lyrics by Oscar Hammerstein II
Music by Richard Rodgers

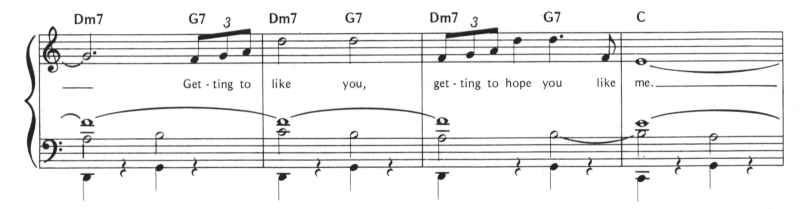

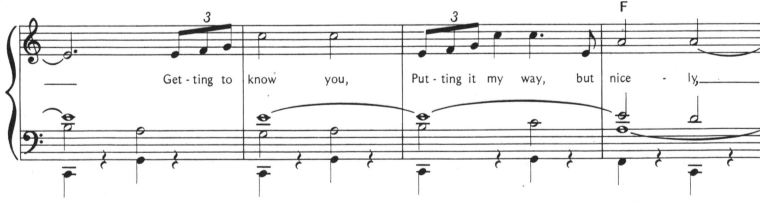

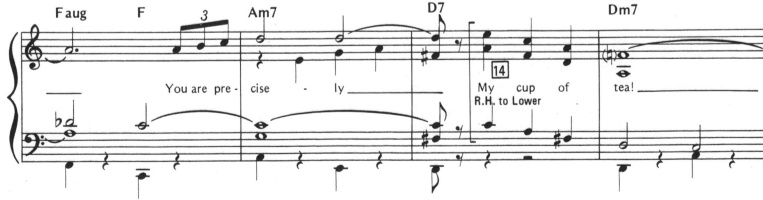

Hello, Young Lovers

from THE KING AND I

Electronic Organs
Upper: Flutes (or Tibias) 16′, 2′
Lower: Flute 8′, 4′, Horn 8′
Pedal: 16′, 8′, Short Sustain
Vib./Trem.: On, Fast

Drawbar Organs
Upper: 80 0400 304
Lower: (00) 7404 203
Pedal: 53
Vib./Trem.: On, Fast

Lyrics by Oscar Hammerstein II
Music by Richard Rodgers

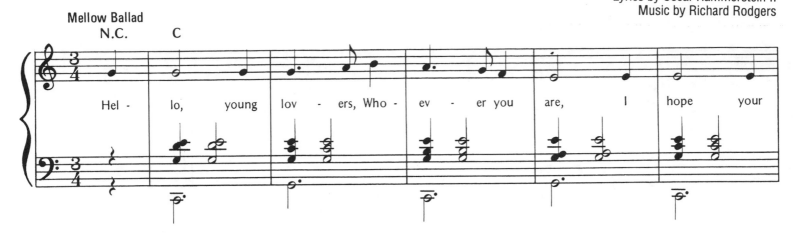

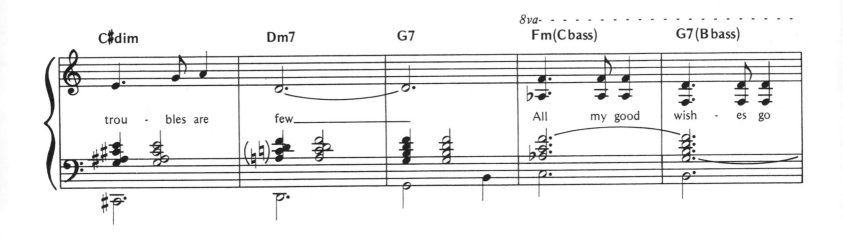

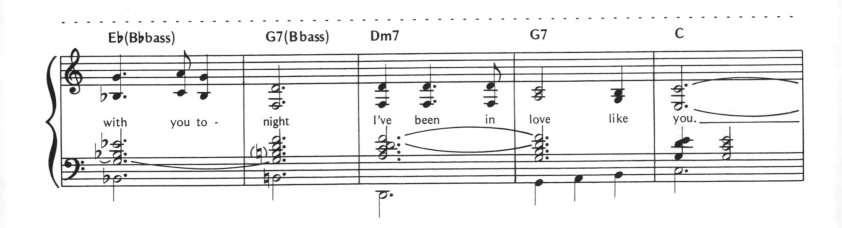

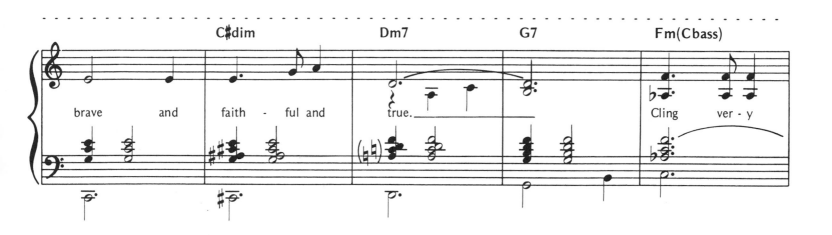

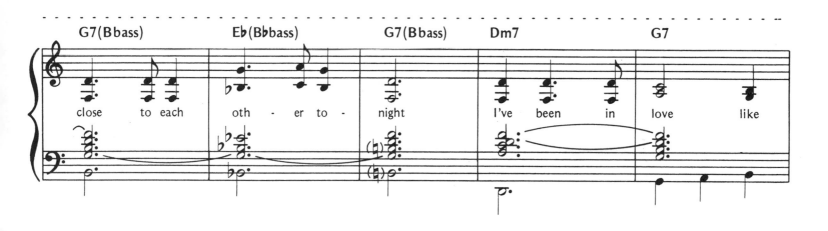

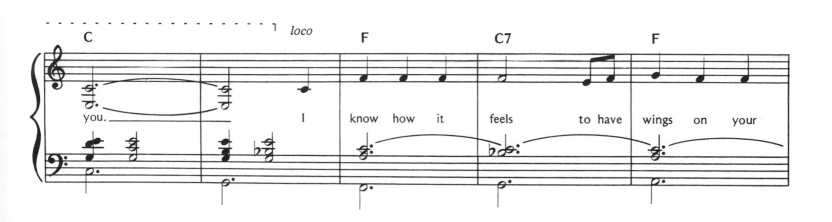

36

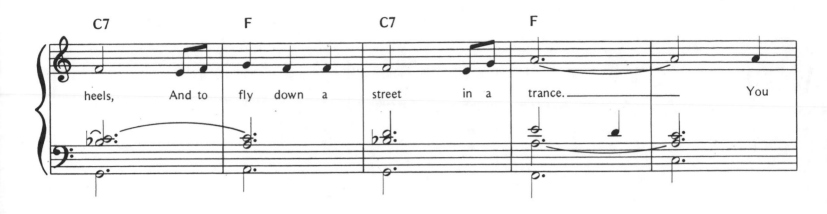

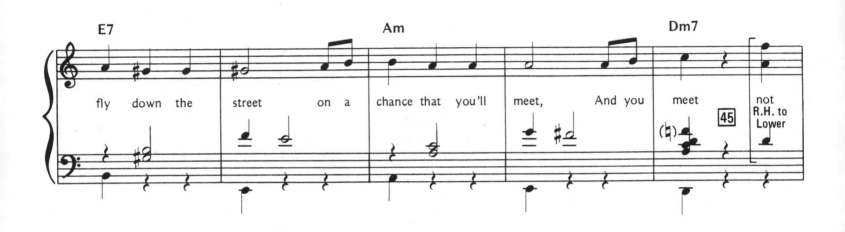

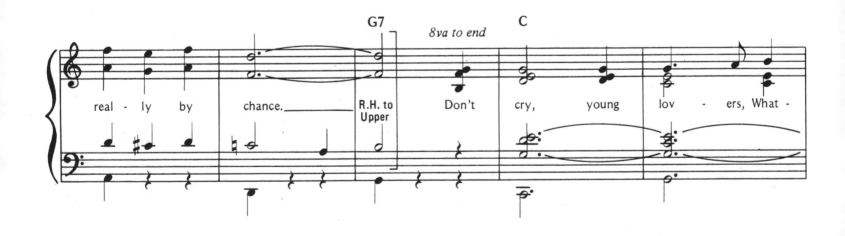

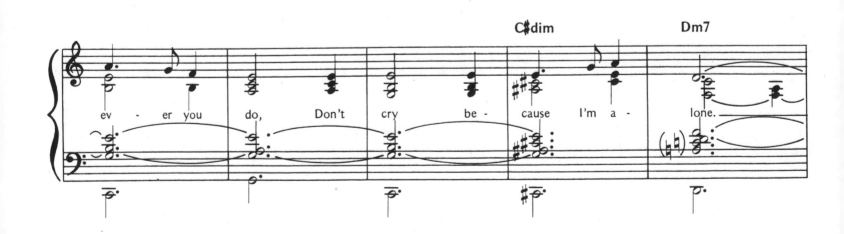

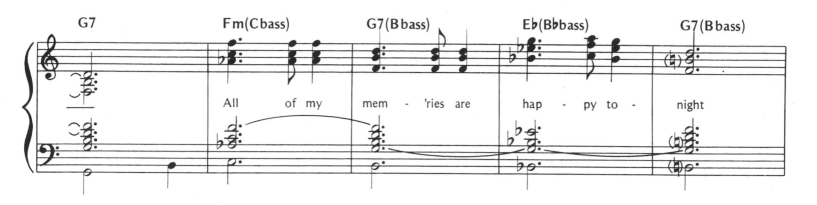

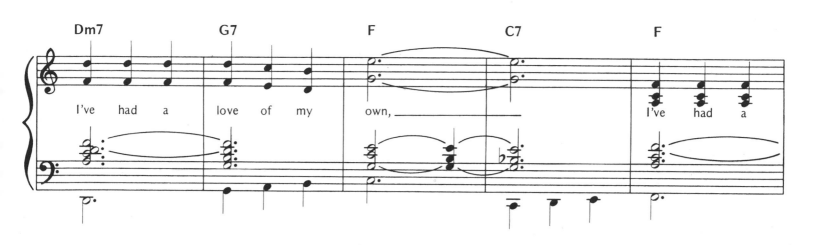

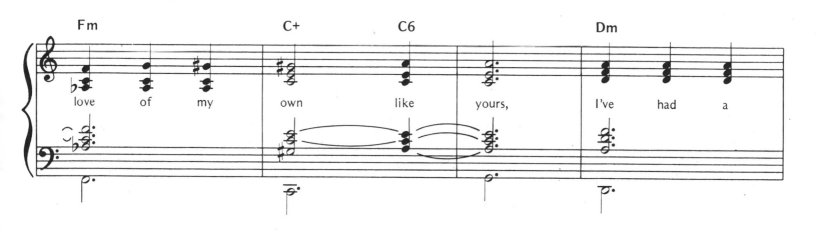

I Could Write a Book

from PAL JOEY

Electronic Organs
Upper: Flutes (or Tibias) 16', 5⅓', 4'
       Clarinet 8'
Lower: Melodia 8', String 4'
Pedal: 16', 8'
Vib./Trem.: On, Fast

Tonebar Organs
Upper: 84 3456 002
Lower: (00) 6456 004
Pedal: 45
Vib./Trem.: On, Fast

Words by Lorenz Hart
Music by Richard Rodgers

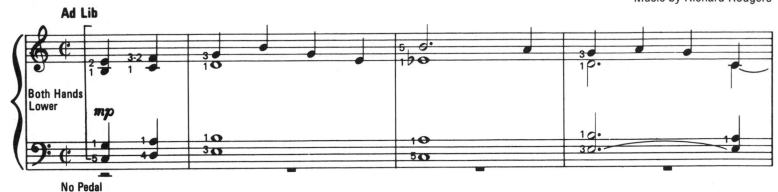

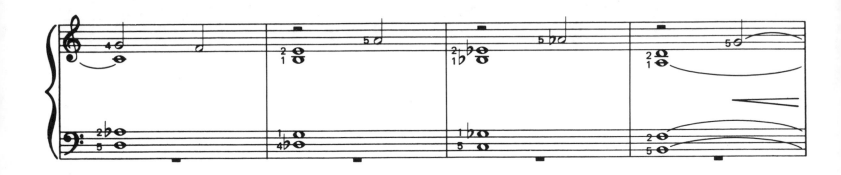

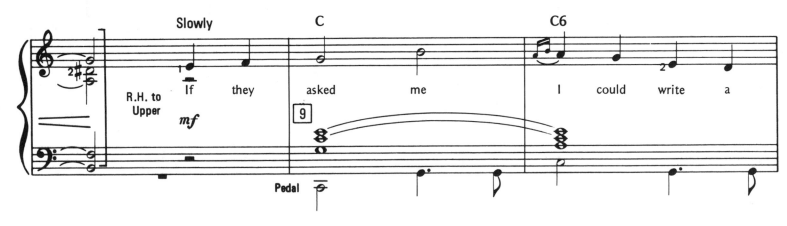

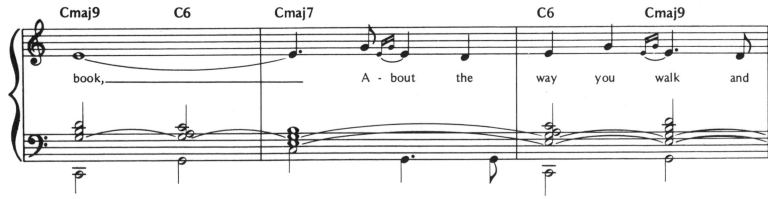

I Love Paris

from CAN-CAN
from HIGH SOCIETY

Electronic Organs
Upper: Flutes (or Tibias) 16', 8', 4'
Lower: Melodia 8', Reed 8'
Pedal: 8'
Vib./Trem.: On, Fast

Tonebar Organs
Upper: 80 4800 000
Lower: (00) 7734 011
Pedal: 44
Vib./Trem.: On, Fast

Words and Music by
Cole Porter

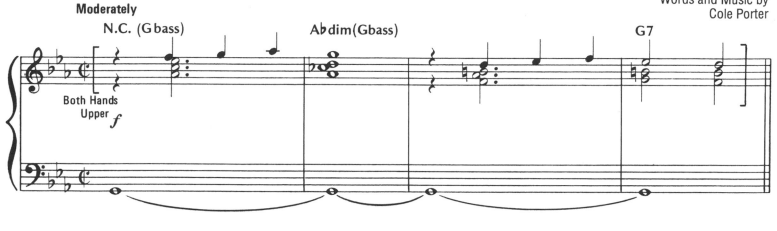

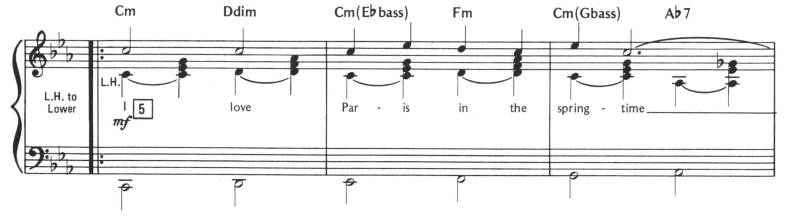

If I Were a Bell

from GUYS AND DOLLS

Electronic Organs

Upper: Preset Piano
Lower: Flutes 8′, 4′
Pedal: String Bass
Vib./Trem.: On, Fast

Drawbar Organs

Preset Piano or
Upper: 80 6606 000
Lower: (00) 7400 000
Pedal: 24
Vib./Trem.: On, Fast

By Frank Loesser

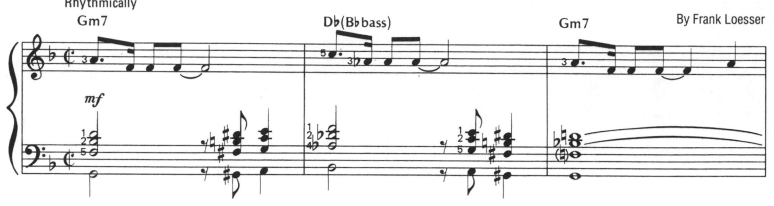

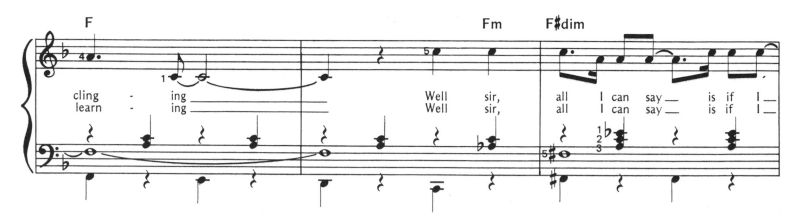

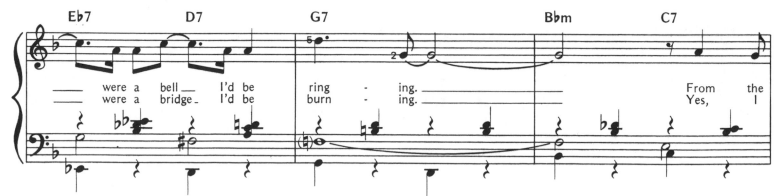

45

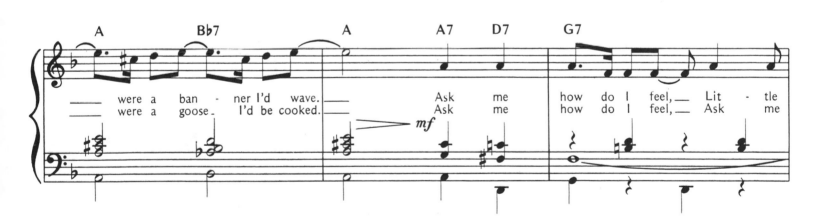

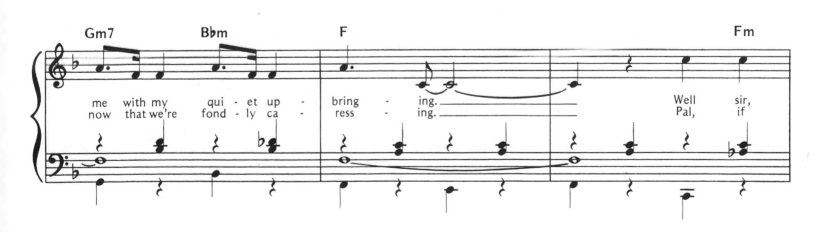

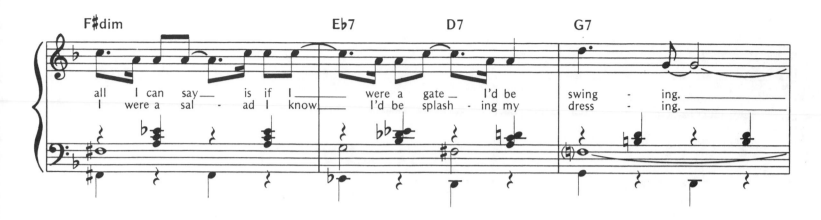

all I can say___ is if I___ were a gate___ I'd be swing - ing. ___
I were a sal - ad I know___ I'd be splash - ing my dress - ing. ___

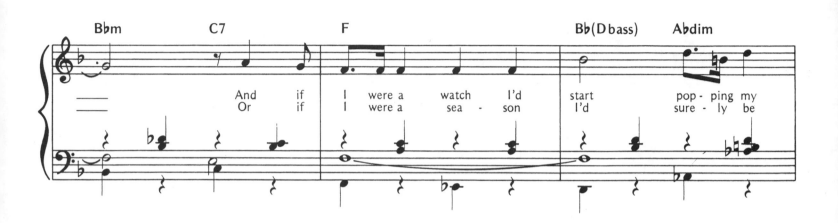

And if I were a watch I'd start pop - ping my
Or if I were a sea - son I'd sure - ly be

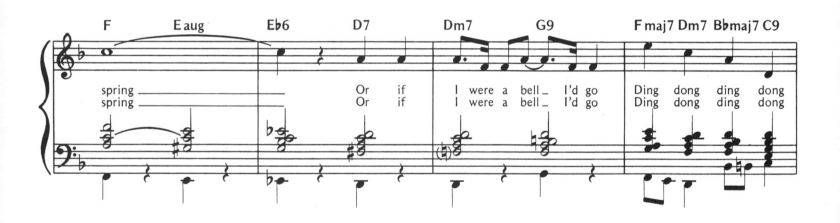

spring ___ Or if I were a bell___ I'd go Ding dong ding dong
spring ___ Or if I were a bell___ I'd go Ding dong ding dong

Ding. Ask me
Ding. ___

Memory

from CATS

Electronic Organs
Upper: Flutes (or Tibias) 16′, 8′,
           4′, 2′
       String 8′
       Clarinet
Lower: Flutes 8′, 4′
Pedal: 16′, 8′
Vib./Trem.: On, Slow

Drawbar Organs
Upper: 80 8104 103
Lower: (00) 6303 004
Pedal: 25
Vib./Trem.: On, Slow

Music by Andrew Lloyd Webber
Text by Trevor Nunn after T.S. Eliot

Lyrics:

Both Hands Lower:
Mid - night. ___ Not a sound from the pave - ment. ___ Has the moon lost her
Mem - 'ry. ___ All a - lone in the moon - light ___ I can smile at the

mem - 'ry? ___ She is smil - ing a - lone. ___ In the
old days, ___ I was beau - ti - ful then. ___ I re -

lamp - light the with - ered leaves col - lect at my feet, ___
mem - ber the time I knew what hap - pi - ness was, ___

And the wind be - gins to moan.
Let the mem - 'ry live a - gain.

Oklahoma

from OKLAHOMA!

Electronic Organs
Upper: Flutes (or Tibias) 16', 8', 2'
　　　 Trumpet
Lower: Flute 4', Diapason 8'
　　　 Reed 8'
Pedal: String Bass
Vib./Trem.: On, Fast

Drawbar Organs
Upper:　80　6368 006
Lower:　(00) 8365 002
Pedal:　String Bass
Vib./Trem.: On, Fast

Lyrics by Oscar Hammerstein II
Music by Richard Rodgers

Moderately, Fast

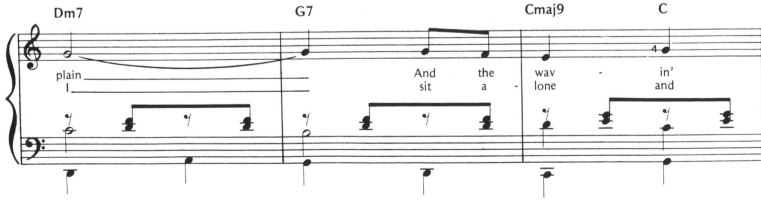

One

from A CHORUS LINE

Electronic Organs
Upper: Flutes (or Tibias) 16′, 8′, 4′, 2′
        Strings 8′, 4′
        Trumpet
Lower: Flutes 8′, 4′, Strings 8′, 4′
        Reed 8′
Pedal: 16′, 8′
Vib./Trem.: On, Fast

Drawbar Organs
Upper: 80 7105 123
Lower: (00) 7314 003
Pedal: 25
Vib./Trem.: On, Fast

Music by Marvin Hamlisch
Lyric by Edward Kleban

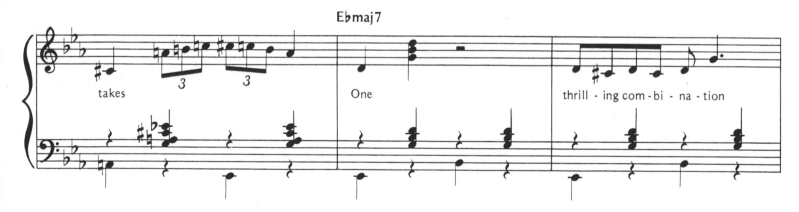

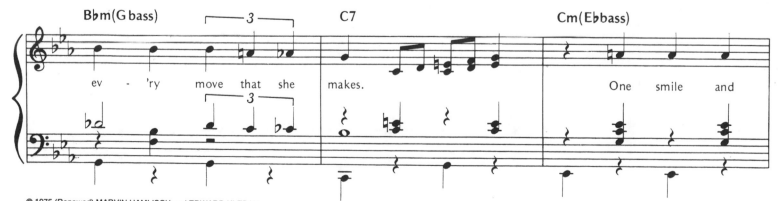

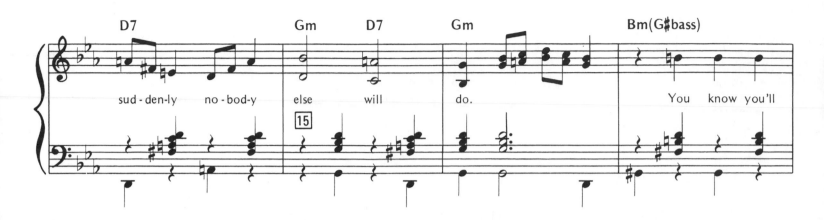

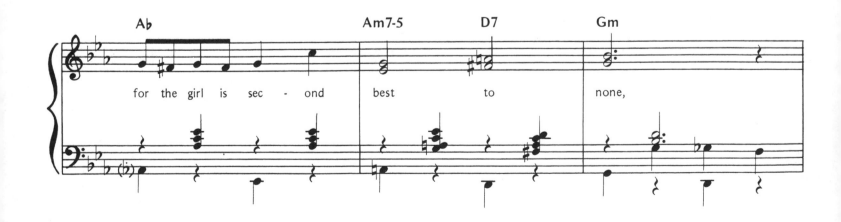

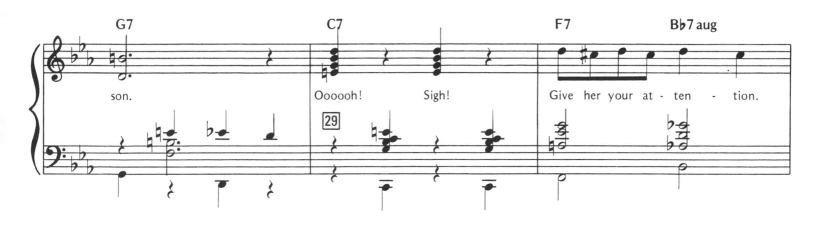

son. Ooooooh! Sigh! Give her your at - ten - tion.

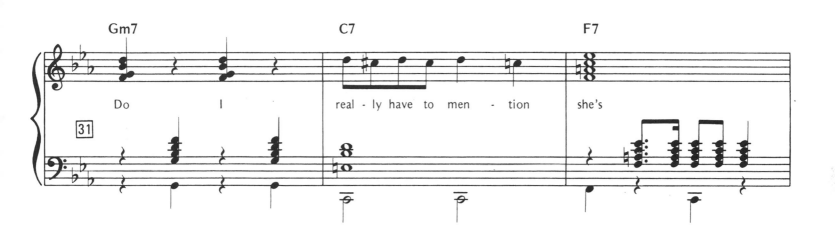

Do I real - ly have to men - tion she's

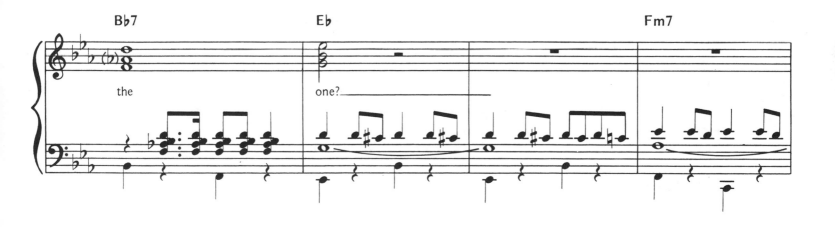

the one? _____

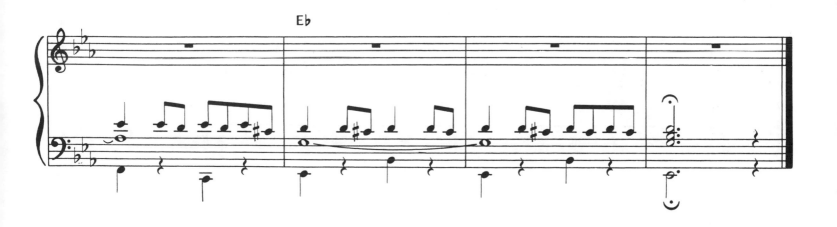

People

from FUNNY GIRL

Electronic Organs

Upper:	Flutes (or Tibias) 8', 4'
Lower:	Horn 8', String 8'
Pedal:	16', Sustain
Vib./Trem:	On, Slow

Drawbar Organs

Upper:	00 7405 000
Lower:	(00) 6787 542
Pedal:	50, Sustain
Vib./Trem.:	On, Slow

Words by Bob Merrill
Music by Jule Styne

The Sound of Music

from THE SOUND OF MUSIC

Electronic Organs
Upper: Flute (or Tibia) 8', Diapason 8',
        String 8'
Lower: Flutes 8', 4'
Pedal: 8'
Vib./Trem.: On, Fast

Drawbar Organs
Upper: 30 8320 000
Lower: (00) 6501 000
Pedal: 24
Vib./Trem.: On, Fast

Lyrics by Oscar Hammerstein II
Music by Richard Rodgers

Speak Low

from the Musical Production ONE TOUCH OF VENUS

Electronic Organs

Upper: String 16', Flutes (or Tibias)
           8', 2 2/3', 2'
Lower: Flutes 8', 4'
Pedal: 16', 8', Sustain
Vib./Trem: On

Drawbar Organs

Upper: 57 8507 000
Lower: (00) 5643 300
Pedal: 42, Sustain
Vib./Trem.: On

Words by Ogden Nash
Music by Kurt Weill

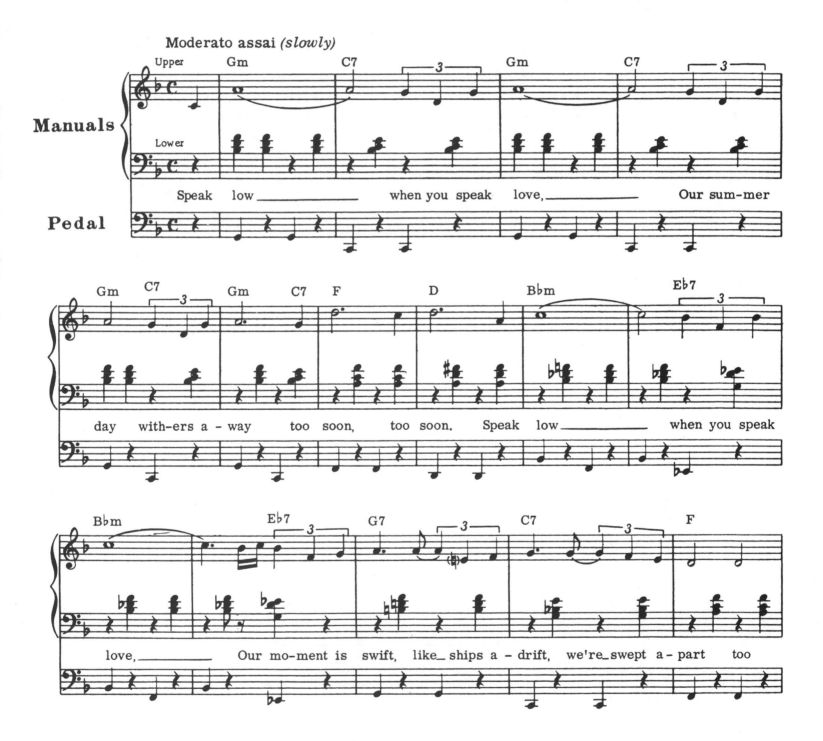

The Surrey with the Fringe on Top

from OKLAHOMA!

Electronic Organs

Upper: Flutes (or Tibias) 16', 4'
Lower: Flute 8', Diapason 8'
Pedal: 8'
Vib./Trem.: On, Slow

Drawbar Organs

Upper: 80 0800 000
Lower: (00) 6405 000
Pedal: 24
Vib./Trem.: On, Slow

Lyrics by Oscar Hammerstein II
Music by Richard Rodgers

Chicks and ducks and geese bet-ter scur-ry
Watch that fringe and see how it flut-ters

When I take you out in the sur - rey,
When I drive them out high step-pin' strut-ters.

When I take you
Nos - ey pokes - 'll

out in the sur - rey with the fringe
peek thru their shut-ters and their eyes

on top! ___
will

There Is Nothin' Like a Dame

from SOUTH PACIFIC

Electronic Organs

Upper: Flutes (or Tibias) 16', 8', 4'
      String 8', Oboe, Trombone
Lower: Flute 8', Diapason 8', String 8',
      Reed 8'
Pedal: String Bass
Vib./Trem.: On, Fast

Drawbar Organs

Upper: 80 7003 051
Lower: (00) 7303 004
Pedal: String Bass
Vib./Trem.: On, Fast

Lyrics by Oscar Hammerstein II
Music by Richard Rodgers

Brightly

We got
sun - light on the sand, we got moon - light on the sea, we got
pack - ag - es from home, we get mo - vies, we get shows, we get
lone - ly, and we long for the fair and gen - tle sex, we would

man - goes and ba - na - nas you can pick right off a tree, we got
speech - es from our skip - per and ad - vice from Tok - yo Rose, we get
like to feel the feel - ing of some arms a - round our necks, we feel

vol - ley ball and ping pong and a lot of dan - dy games!
let - ters doused with per - fume, we get diz - zy from the smell!
hun - gry as the wolf felt when he met Red Rid - ing Hood.

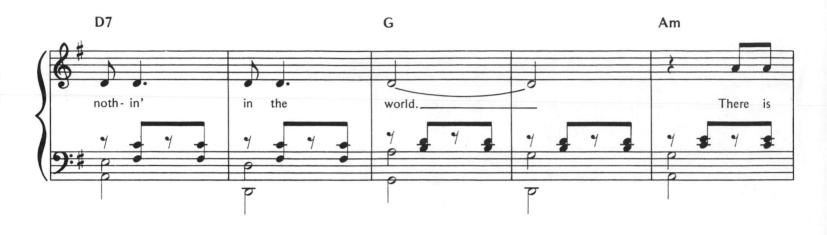

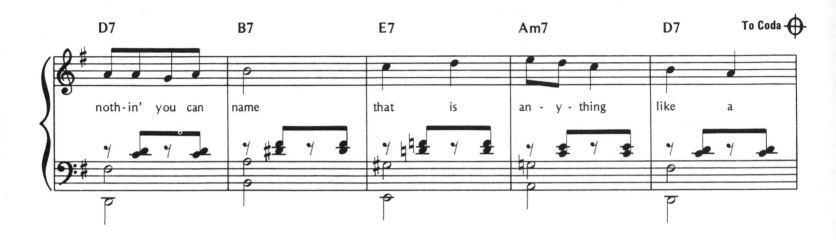

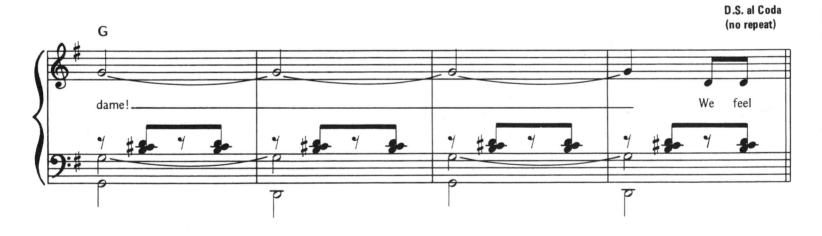

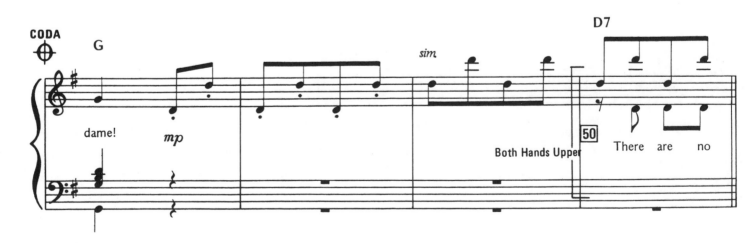

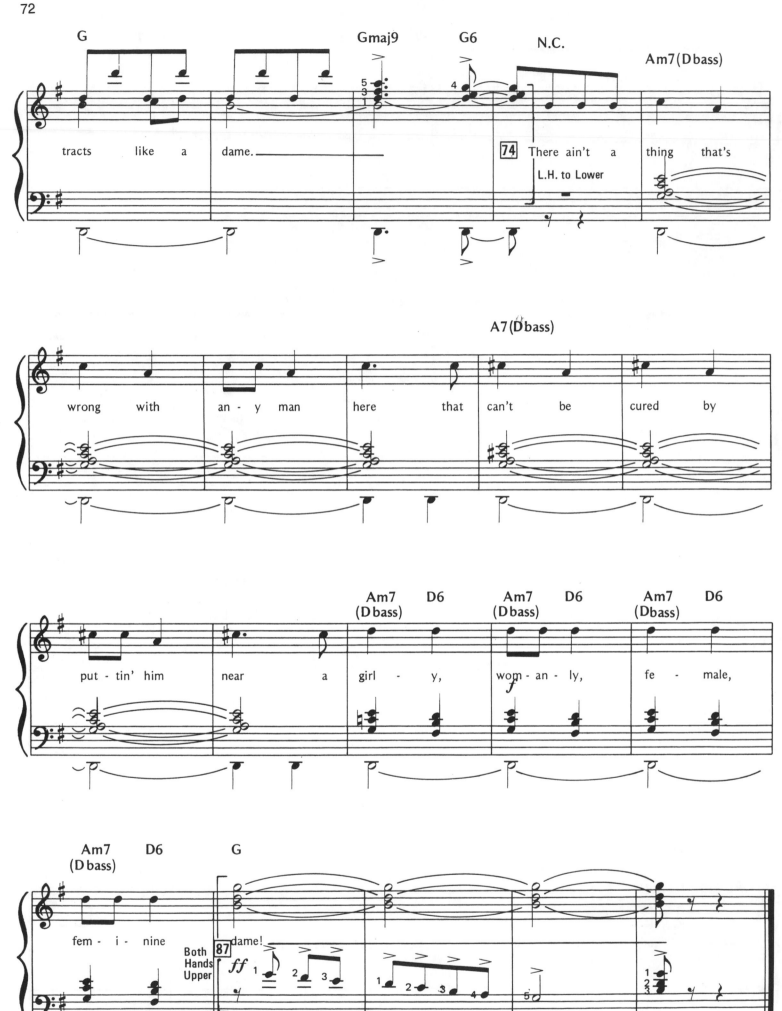

Tomorrow

from the Musical Production ANNIE

Electronic Organs

Upper: Flutes (or Tibias) 16′, 8′, 2′
       Trumpet
Lower: Flute 4′, Diapason 8′, Reed 8′
Pedal: String Bass
Vib./Trem.: On, Fast

Drawbar Organs

Upper: 80 6368 006
Lower: (00) 8365 002
Pedal: String Bass
Vib./Trem.: On, Fast

Lyric by Martin Charnin
Music by Charles Strouse

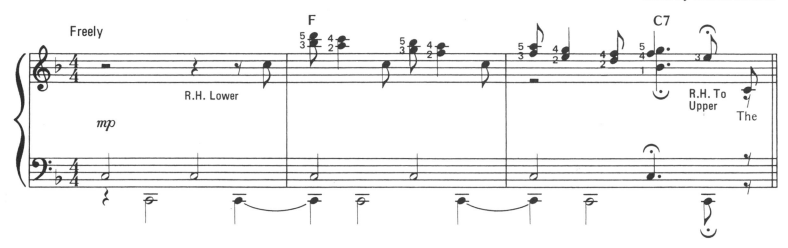

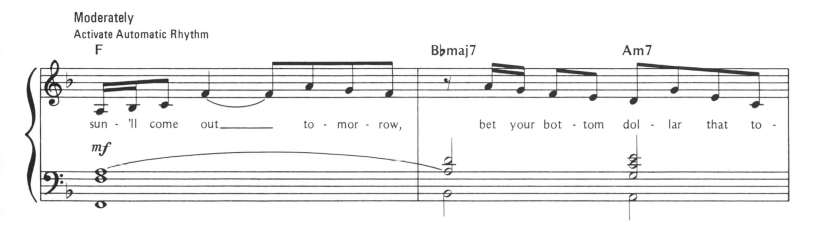

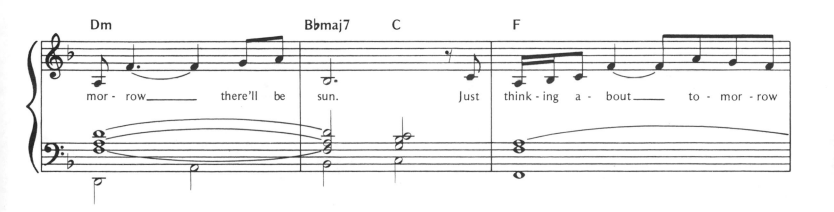

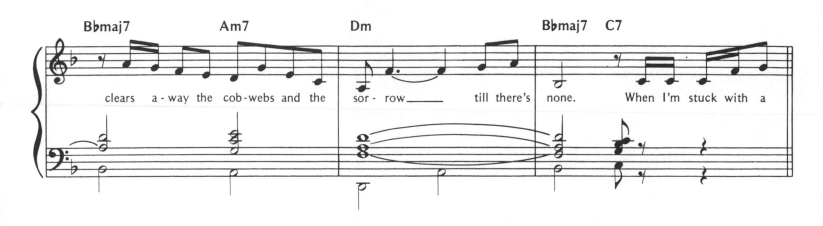

clears a-way the cob-webs and the sor-row ____ till there's none. When I'm stuck with a

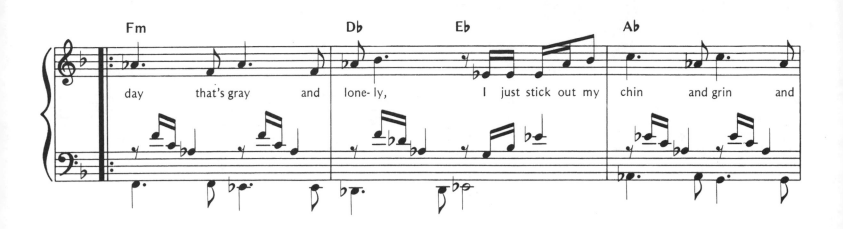

day that's gray and lone-ly, I just stick out my chin and grin and

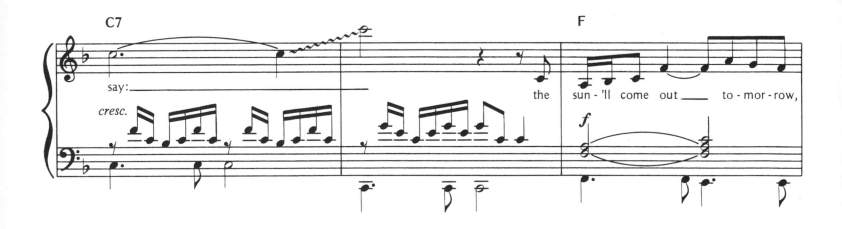

say: ____ the sun-'ll come out ____ to-mor-row,

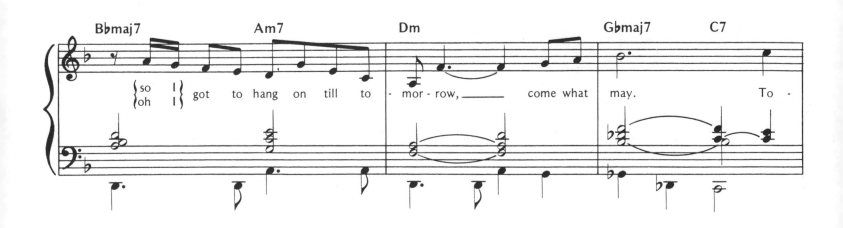

{so / oh} got to hang on till to-mor-row, ____ come what may. To-

There's No Business Like Show Business

from the Stage Production ANNIE GET YOUR GUN

Electronic Organs
Upper: Flutes (or Tibias) 8', 4', 2'
       Trombone, Trumpet, Clarinet (16')
Lower: Flute 8', String 8', Reed 8'
Pedal: 16', 8'
Vib./Trem.: On, Fast

Tonebar Organs
Upper: 82 5864 200
Lower: (00) 7103 000
Pedal: 45
Vib./Trem.: On, Fast

Words and Music by
Irving Berlin

Brightly

THE BEST SELECTION OF ORGAN MUSIC AVAILABLE

21 Contemporary Love & Wedding Songs
Includes: All I Ask of You • Endless Love • Forever and Ever, Amen • Friends • Just the Way You Are • Somewhere Out There • Too Much Heaven • Woman • You Needed Me • and more.
00290108 . . . . $8.95

50 Standards for Organ
50 favorite standards: Autumn Leaves • The Christmas Song • Hello, Dolly! • I Wanna Be Loved by You • A Good Man Is Hard to Find • Sentimental Journey • One • Unchained Melody • What I Did for Love • Witchcraft • and more.
00290291 . . . . $12.95

All-Time Standards
25 of the best-loved songs of all time: All of Me • Fly Me to the Moon (In Other Words) • Gigi • I've Grown Accustomed to Her Face • My Funny Valentine • Stompin' at the Savoy • Tuxedo Junction • and more.
00199015 . . . . $9.95

Irving Berlin Favorites for Organ
arr. Dan Rodowicz
23 Berlin favorites, including: Always • Blue Skies • Happy Holiday • I've Got My Love to Keep Me Warm • Puttin' On the Ritz • and many more.
00290251 . . . . $9.95

Best Songs Ever for Organ
Over 70 must-own classics: All I Ask of You • Crazy • Endless Love • Fly Me to the Moon • In the Mood • Love Me Tender • My Funny Valentine • People • Somewhere Out There • Strangers in the Night • Tears in Heaven • A Time for Us • The Way We Were • When I Fall in Love • and more.
00199060 . . . . $19.95

Big Band & Swing
Relive the dance hall days with this great collection of 25 swingin' favorites: All or Nothing at All • Basin Street Blues • Manhattan • Mood Indigo • Paper Doll • Route 66 • Sentimental Journey • Stormy Weather (Keeps Rainin' All the Time) • and more.
00199010 . . . . $9.95

Contemporary Christian Classics
12 beloved songs arranged for organ. Music and lyrics are provided for such classics as: Behold the Lamb • El Shaddai • How Majestic Is Your Name • Upon This Rock • We Shall Behold Him • and many more.
00199100 . . . . $6.95

Country Classics
25 must-own country standards: Crazy • Crying in the Chapel • Deep in the Heart of Texas • Folsom Prison Blues • King of the Road • Make the World Go Away • Somebody's Knockin' • Wabash Cannonball • and more.
00199013 . . . . $9.95

Disney Hits
12 big Disney hits arranged for organ: Be Our Guest • Beauty and the Beast • Can You Feel the Love Tonight • Colors of the Wind • God Help the Outcasts • Hakuna Matata • A Whole New World • You'll Be in My Heart • and more.
00199008 . . . . $10.95

Easy Classics
arr. Jim Cliff
12 titles for easy organ: Chopin's Nocturne • Emperor Waltz • Jesu, Joy of Man's Desiring • Ode to Joy (from Beethoven's Ninth Symphony) • Vienna Life • and others.
00276400 . . . . $5.95

Great Standards for Organ
50 timeless songs: All at Once You Love Her • Call Me • The Entertainer • I Could Write a Book • I'll Be Around • My Romance • Ol' Man River • Smoke Gets in Your Eyes • Why Do I Love You? • Younger Than Springtime • and many more.
00290207 . . . . $12.95

Latin Organ Favorites
Over 20 Latin favorites, including: Desafinado • The Girl from Ipanema • How Insensitive • More • One Note Samba • Quiet Nights Of Quiet Stars • and more.
00199107 . . . . $9.95

Les Misérables Selections for Organ
14 songs from this smash hit musical including: Bring Him Home • Castle on a Cloud • Do You Hear the People Sing? • I Dreamed a Dream • In My Life • On My Own • and more. Also includes color photos from the Broadway production.
00290270 . . . . $12.95

Phantom of the Opera
9 of the best songs from the smash hit musical, including: All I Ask of You • Think of Me • Wishing You Were Somehow Here Again • and more.
00290300 . . . . $14.95

Pop Classics
25 top hits, including: Can't Help Falling in Love • Every Breath You Take • Hopelessly Devoted to You • Islands in the Stream • Let It Be • Unchained Melody • We've Only Just Begun • You Needed Me • and more.
00199012 . . . . $9.95

The Rodgers & Hammerstein All-Organ Book
Over 40 songs from hit Broadway shows, including: Oklahoma! • State Fair • Allegro • South Pacific • The King and I • Pipe Dream • Flower Drum Song • Cinderella • The Sound of Music.
00312899 . . . . $12.95

Showtunes
25 favorites from the stage: Bewitched • Blue Skies • Cabaret • Edelweiss • Get Me to the Church on Time • Getting to Know You • Memory • Oklahoma • One • People • The Surrey with the Fringe on Top • Tomorrow • and more.
00199009 . . . . $9.95

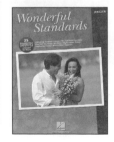

Wonderful Standards
Take a trip down memory lane with these 25 gems: After You've Gone • Bluesette • Body and Soul • The Girl from Ipanema (Garota De Ipanema) • I've Got You Under My Skin • So Nice (Summer Samba) • Younger Than Springtime • and more.
00199011 . . . . $9.95